Teaching Little Fingers to Play
More Recital Pieces

Piano Solos with Optional Teacher Accompaniments
by
Carolyn Miller

CONTENTS

Cover Art by Nick Gressle

Book
ISBN-13: 978-1-4234-0804-8

Book/CD
ISBN-13: 978-1-4234-0811-6

WILLIS MUSIC

EXCLUSIVELY DISTRIBUTED BY

HAL•LEONARD®
CORPORATION
7777 W. BLUEMOUND RD. P.O. BOX 13819 MILWAUKEE, WI 53213

Visit Hal Leonard Online at
www.halleonard.com

Let's Rock
Optional Teacher Accompaniment

Carolyn Miller

With energy ♩ = *100-116*

Let's Rock

Play both hands one octave higher when performing as a duet.

Carolyn Miller

With energy ♩ = 100 - 116

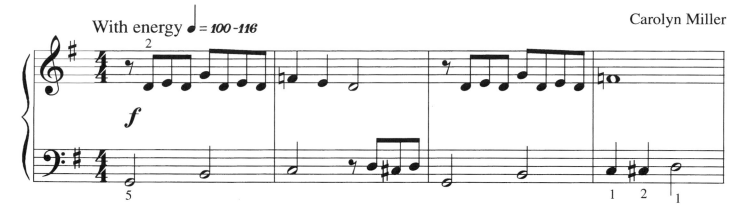

Happy Day
Optional Teacher Accompaniment

Carolyn Miller

Happy Day

Play both hands one octave higher when performing as a duet.

Carolyn Miller

Optional Teacher Accompaniment

The Boatman
Optional Teacher Accompaniment

Carolyn Miller

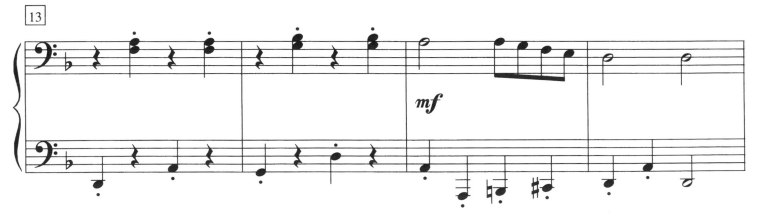

The Boatman

Play both hands one octave higher when performing as a duet.

Carolyn Miller

Optional Teacher Accompaniment

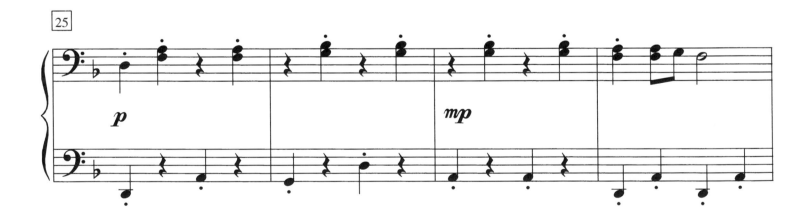

L.H. over

Recital Waltz
Optional Teacher Accompaniment

Carolyn Miller

Moderato ♩ = 125

Recital Waltz

Play both hands one octave higher when performing as a duet.

Moderato ♩= *125*

Carolyn Miller

mf

Optional Teacher Accompaniment

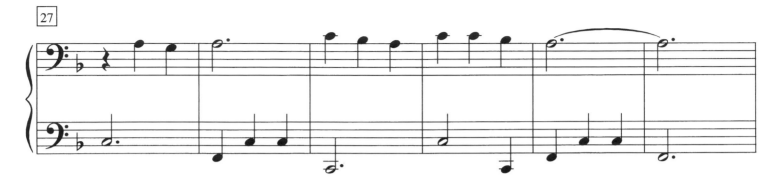

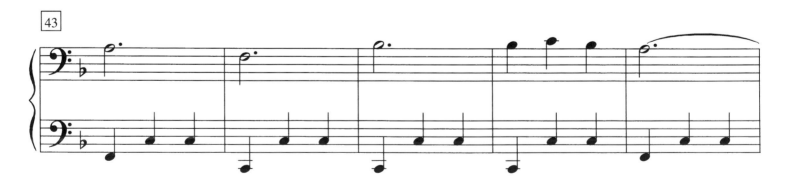

1 2 1

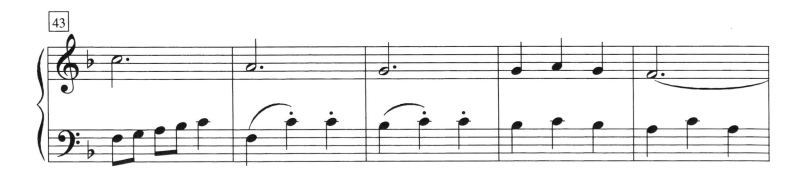

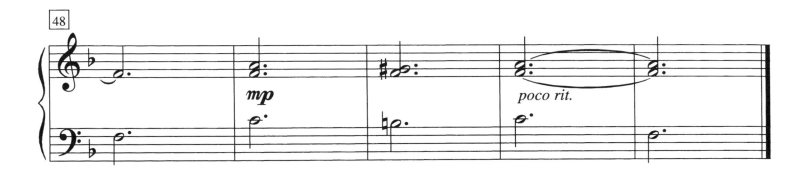

Mystery
Optional Teacher Accompaniment

Carolyn Miller

Mystery

Carolyn Miller

Play both hands one octave higher when performing as a duet.

Misterioso ♩ = 120

1. *To next strain* | *Fine*

L.H. over

Optional Teacher Accompaniment

D.C. al Fine

It's Cool
Optional Teacher Accompaniment

Carolyn Miller

It's Cool

Play both hands one octave higher when performing as a duet.

Carolyn Miller

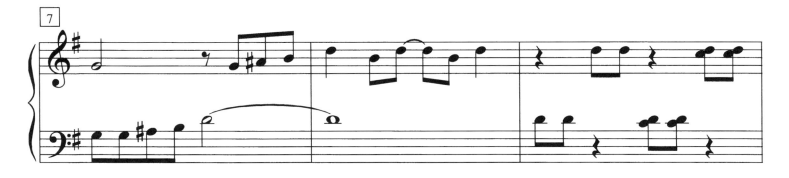

Optional Teacher Accompaniment

23